FESTIVALS IN SCOTLAND

By Frances Jarvie

Illustrated by Fhiona Galloway

Edinburgh : HMSO
National Museums of Scotland

Festivals in Scotland

A wealth of different festivals and gatherings in Scotland take place throughout the year. From exotic fire festivals, or blessing a fishing fleet, to a local gala queen being crowned, we all celebrate some of them, whether we live in the country, by the sea, or in a village, town or city.

Festivals are a way of remembering times past, who we are and where we belong. They add colour, and enrich our lives as each wave of peoples has brought their customs and beliefs to our shores.

Many festivals are based on the seasons, as this is how the Celtic peoples divided their year. Often festivities took place on a hill-top, or there was a procession around a sacred well. Long ago, these were the few times when people could relax from their daily toil and enjoy games, dances and markets. For a short while they could forget their dependence on the seasons.

In the Middle Ages the burghs were allowed to hold annual fairs where country folk would enjoy the story-tellers, acrobats, minstrels and other entertainers – the forerunners of our town and city festivals today. The church also had many saints' days which gave another welcome break in the routine. Many ancient customs have survived and are now blended with our present Christian festivals.

Many of our traditions, customs and even superstitions are kept alive when we celebrate – so join in, have fun and keep them going for the future!

DECEMBER
St. Nicholas Festival~ Aberdeen ○ Christmas ○ Swinging the Fire Balls Stonehaven○ Flambeaux Procession○ Comrie○ Hogmanay

JANUARY
New Year's Day ○ Ba' Games~Orkney○ Scalloway Fire Festival~Shetland Burning of the Clavie~Burghead Burns Night Up Helly Aa~ Lerwick

FEBRUARY
Candlemas~ Scottish Quarter Day○ Borders Hand~Ba' Games Chinese New Year

MARCH
Whuppity Stourie~Lanark

APRIL
April Fool's Day (Hunt the Gowk) ○ Easter○ Kate Kennedy Procession ~ St. Andrews Links Market Kirkcaldy○ Atholl Highland Gathering

MAY
Beltane May day Mayfest~Glasgow St.Magnus Festival~ Orkney○ Bon Accord Festival○ Aberdeen Ceres Festival○ Melrose Festival○ Beltane Week~Peebles○ Galashiels Gathering○ Riding of the Marches

JUNE
Riding of the Marches○ Eyemouth○ St.Monans Sea Queen Festival○ of the Herring Queen○ Ride~Kelso○ Yetholm○ Jedburgh○ Callants' Festival○ Reiver's Week~Duns

JULY
St.Andrews Lammas Fair~ Scottish Quarter Day Cleikum St.Ronans Folk Festival○ Lossiemouth Festival○ Fraserburgh Fish Festival○ Dundee City Fest.

AUGUST
Argyllshire Gathering~Oban○ Aberdeen Fish Festival○ Pittenweem Festival○ The Burryman~South Queensferry○ Edinburgh International Festival○

SEPTEMBER
Michaelmas Largs Viking Festival Fisherman's Walk~Musselburgh Blairgowrie Highland Games Braemar Gathering

OCTOBER
Hallowe'en Harvest Festivals

NOVEMBER
Martinmas~Scottish Quarter Day St Andrew's Day

HOGMANAY – 31 DECEMBER

Our mid-winter festivals have survived since Celtic times and were celebrated to hasten the return of the sun. In the past thirty years our Christmas, Hogmanay and New Year have become an extended celebration, taking us back to the original Yuletide or Twelve Days of Christmas.

Hogmanay comes from a French dialect word *hoguinane* which was a song sung by children going from door to door for gifts:

We no longer have guisers on New Year's Eve, but certain customs live on. Fireworks, street carnivals, ceilidhs and ringing out the old year are some of the public events to celebrate the onset of New Year.

There are different traditions throughout Scotland on 31 December. In Comrie, Perthshire, there is a Flambeaux Procession through the village to ward off evil spirits. The enormous flaming torches are lit just before midnight before being paraded through Comrie.

At Stonehaven there is the Fireball Ceremony. Blazing fireballs are swung above the bearers' heads to greet the New Year

and bring prosperity to the town. Both these fire festivals can be traced back to an age when the power of the sun was worshipped.

On the night of Auld Hogmanay (11 January) at Burghead on the Moray Firth they celebrate the Burning of the Clavie. The clavie is a barrel filled with tar, which is ignited and carried around the streets to burn out the old year. It is then taken to a headland hill, more fuel is piled on and finally burning pieces of the barrel are seized as good luck tokens for the rest of the year.

As the Old Year is burnt out, or rung out, the New Year begins – but not without all of its own superstitions in Scotland!

At some point over the New Year festivities you will be encouraged to sing Auld Lang Syne by Robert Burns. Do you know the words?

New Year – 1 January

A guid New Year to yin and a'! And mony may ye see,
And during a' the years to come, O happy may ye be.

A hundred years ago New Year's Day was the only holiday in Scotland which servants and other workers had in the winter. Christmas was just another working day, in comparison to the ancient rituals celebrated at New Year.

It was important that the house was cleaned thoroughly and all the chores up to date. After midnight we still enjoy the custom of first-footing which comes from the good fairy of Norse folklore. Scots believe that their 'first-foot' gives luck to the household for the following year. The first-foot should preferably be male, tall and dark – a red-haired woman, or anyone with flat feet or cross-eyes is considered very unlucky!

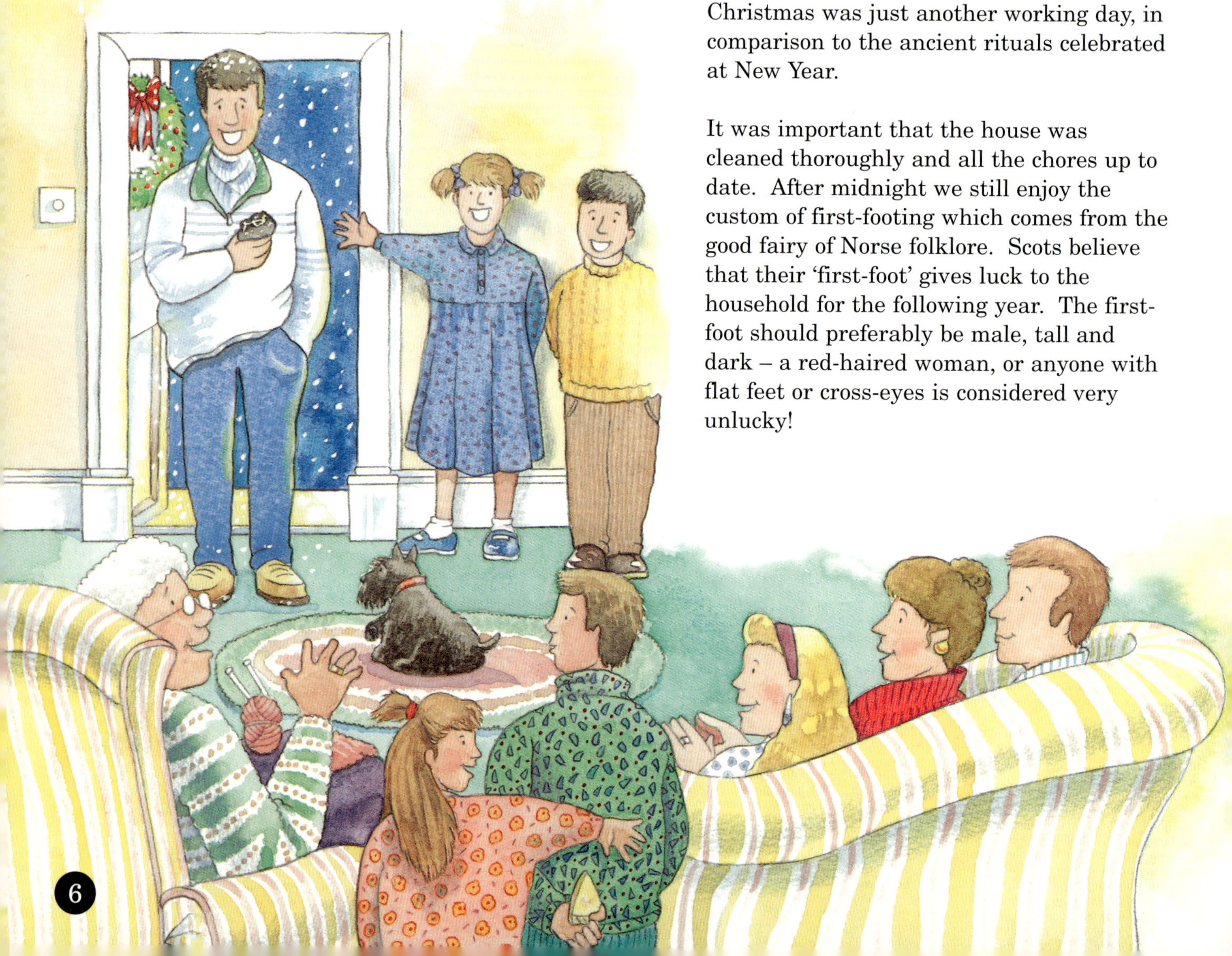

Certain gifts are given as people first-foot – representing the time when the clergy took food and wine to the poor. Nowadays we traditionally present shortbread or Scotch Bun and offer a New Year drink. Until recently a piece of coal would be given to symbolise wishing warmth to the household and salt to represent wealth.

Try making your own shortbread, traditionally associated with New Year. The large round biscuit comes from the ancient Yule Bannock, notched around the edge to represent the sun's rays.

You will need: *250g / 8oz butter*
125g / 4oz sugar
375g / 12oz plain white flour

1. Work the butter until soft in the mixing bowl.

2. Mix in the sugar until creamy.

3. Mix in the flour using hands. Knead lightly until smooth. Leave it until it is a little firmer and easy to roll.

4. Divide the mixture in two and roll out 2 circles, each 1 to 1.5 cm thick.

5. Flute the edges and mark with a knife into 8 sections. Prick with a fork and place on lightly greased baking tray.

6. Bake in a moderate oven, Gas 4; 350°F or 180°C for 30 minutes until straw-coloured and firm.

7. Dust the top with caster sugar whilst hot.

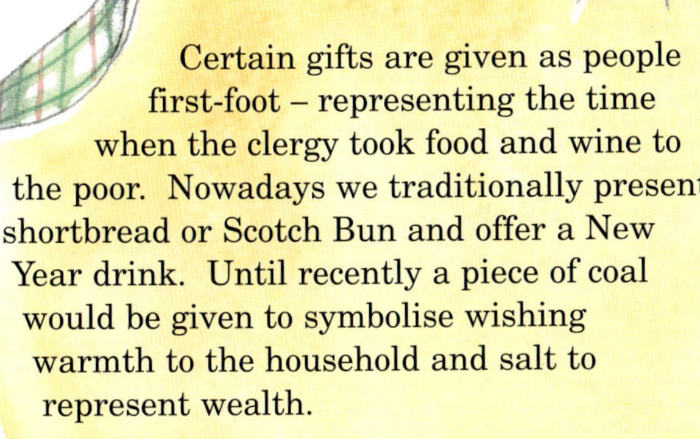

BURNS NIGHT – 25 JANUARY

This is the birthday of Scotland's much-loved National Bard, the poet Robert Burns (1759-96). Within a few years of his death, Burns Clubs were being formed to celebrate the poet's life and work, and to encourage people to read his poetry. By the time of the centenary of Burns's birth in 1859, the idea of an annual Burns Supper was well established – not just in the poet's home counties of Ayrshire and Dumfriesshire, but in Scots communities throughout the world.

The format of a Burns Supper follows a long-established ritual: Dinner, then Speeches, then Songs and Recitations. Guests are often asked to include an item of tartan in their dress for the evening. A typical menu is as follows:

The highlight of the dinner occurs when the chef brings the haggis into the dining room, usually to a bagpipe or fiddle accompaniment and the slow handclapping of the guests, as it is ceremoniously marched up to the top table.

Bill o' Fare

Some hae meat and canna eat
And some wad eat that want it :
But we hae meat and we can eat,
And sae the Lord be thankit.
(The Selkirk Grace)

Cock-a-leekie Soup

Haggis ~ warm, reekin, rich wi
champit tatties and bashed neeps

Address to the Haggis

Poached Salmon

Tipsy Laird

A Tassie o' Coffee

The Chairman of the event then recites 'To a Haggis', one of Burns's most famous poems, and performs the 'slaying' ceremony as he reads the third verse.

After the dinner the principal speaker rises to deliver 'The Immortal Memory', which is the main speech of the evening. This aims to make all the guests want to read or re-read the poetry of Burns. A male speaker then offers a 'Toast to the Lassies' and a female speaker replies. Various other toasts and speeches may be added before the singing, recitations, or sometimes dancing, begins.

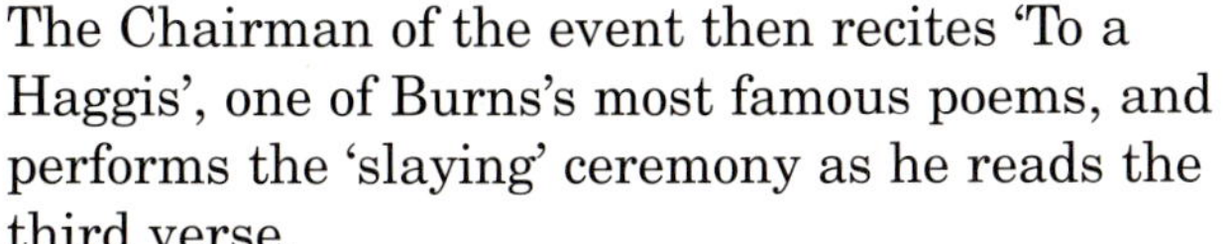

Can you perform any Burns recitations? You could easily learn a poem or a song, like 'The Banks o' Doon' or 'A Red, Red Rose' or 'To a Mouse'. Recitations are useful not just for Burns Suppers, but for performance at Hogmanay or Hallowe'en.

Up-Helly-Aa – January

One of the finest fire-festivals in Europe is held at Lerwick in Shetland. It marks the end of the Yule festivities – the end of the holy days – and takes place in late January.

Shetland is as near to Norway as it is to Aberdeen, so Shetlanders still have close links with their Norse neighbours and their Viking history. It was the Norse custom to place their dead Viking chiefs in a longship and set it on fire to send them to Valhalla – the Viking heaven. Orkney and Shetland were once conquered by Viking pirates. The islands were used for violent raids on the mainland.

Today a replica of a longship is built. It is led through the streets by a ceremonial chief, Guiser Jarl, who is the main figure throughout the festivities. Guiser Jarl and his crew are accompanied by a magnificent torchlight procession before the galley is burnt by throwing lighted torches into it. There follows a night of carnival, with halls open throughout the town, and dancing and revelry until dawn.

Try to make a model of a Viking longship with a dragon head, heraldic shields on each side and one large sail, attached to a cross-pole on the mast.

LARGS VIKING FESTIVAL – SEPTEMBER

The Battle of Largs was the last Norse raid on the mainland of Scotland. In 1263 the Norwegian King Haakon's fleet was moored in the Firth of Clyde. As the winter neared, a severe storm blew many longships ashore. The Vikings were forced back by the Scots, but set fire to their abandoned longships. The damaged fleet returned to Orkney and King Haakon died at Kirkwall. The Western Isles then became part of Scotland, no longer ruled by a Norse king.

This festival is held at the beginning of September and is a spectacular combination of events. There are Viking Children's Games, based on Viking tests of strength, skill and speed – Thor's Axe Throw; Spear Wrestling; Viking Circle; Sacred Sword Ring; Tug o' War and A Race to Arms. There is story-telling of Viking folktales and a re-enactment of the Battle of Largs, with a longship being consigned to the Gods, followed by a firework display. On the last day there is a torchlight procession, led by a giant figure of a Viking God.

The culture of a distant age lives on in the Largs Viking Centre, open all year.

BA' GAMES

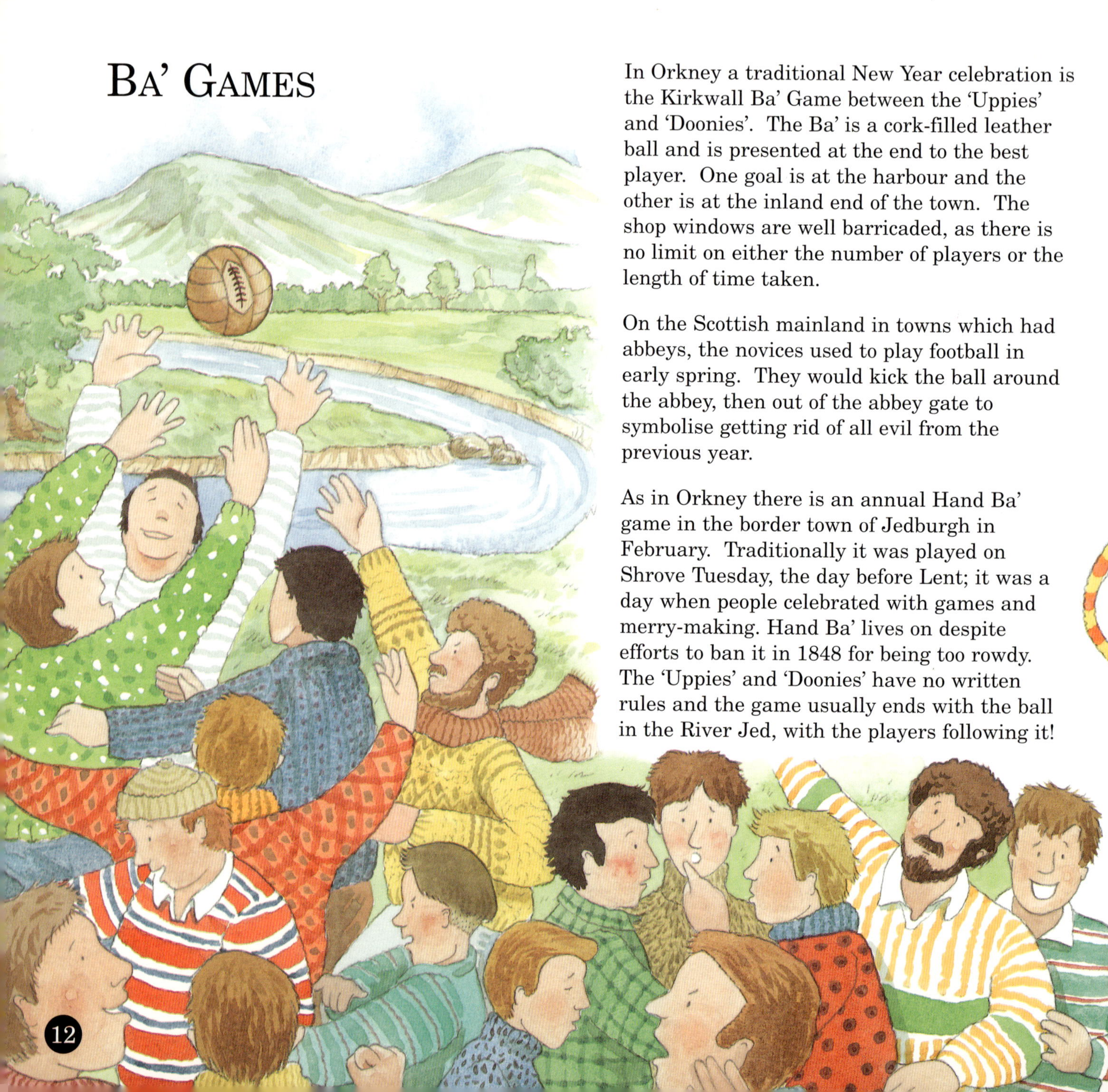

In Orkney a traditional New Year celebration is the Kirkwall Ba' Game between the 'Uppies' and 'Doonies'. The Ba' is a cork-filled leather ball and is presented at the end to the best player. One goal is at the harbour and the other is at the inland end of the town. The shop windows are well barricaded, as there is no limit on either the number of players or the length of time taken.

On the Scottish mainland in towns which had abbeys, the novices used to play football in early spring. They would kick the ball around the abbey, then out of the abbey gate to symbolise getting rid of all evil from the previous year.

As in Orkney there is an annual Hand Ba' game in the border town of Jedburgh in February. Traditionally it was played on Shrove Tuesday, the day before Lent; it was a day when people celebrated with games and merry-making. Hand Ba' lives on despite efforts to ban it in 1848 for being too rowdy. The 'Uppies' and 'Doonies' have no written rules and the game usually ends with the ball in the River Jed, with the players following it!

CHINESE NEW YEAR – JANUARY / FEBRUARY

A recent festival which has come to our cities is the Chinese Spring Festival, or Chinese New Year. There is no fixed date as it depends on the Chinese lunar calendar, but takes place between 21 January and 20 February.

A 12-year cycle is followed as there are 12 new moons in each year, with each year represented by an animal. According to legend, Buddha summoned all the animals in the world to him one New Year, promising them a reward. Only 12 animals obeyed and each of them was given a year. The Rat was first, followed by the Buffalo, Tiger, Cat, Dragon, Snake, Horse, Goat, Monkey, Cockerel, Dog and the Pig. In which animal's year were you born?

As with our New Year, the Chinese New Year is full of symbols to get it off to a good start.

There are traditional foods; gifts of lucky money to children, in red and gold envelopes; special greetings cards and a lion dance in the street, with firecrackers and clashing cymbals. Look out for the next colourful lion dance in Glasgow or Edinburgh at this time of year. No Chinese New Year meal is complete without fish. The Chinese character for 'abundance' sounds the same as 'fish'.

EASTER – MARCH / APRIL

Easter is one of the happiest celebrations of the Christian year. People remember that Jesus triumphed over death, bringing new life to all who follow him. Its date varies because it is kept in original relation to the Passover date which depends on the phases of the moon. The word Easter comes from Eastre, the goddess of light and spring. In many European languages the word for Easter comes from the name Passover – an important Jewish festival:

Eggs are an important part of Easter as they symbolise new life. They were an important part of spring festivals long before Christianity. Today we decorate hard-boiled eggs and roll them downhill to remind us of the stone being rolled aside from Jesus' tomb. Chocolate Easter eggs are given – some are shaped like rabbits.

Originally the Easter hare was the sacred companion of the goddess Eastre. Children were told that the magic hare would run through the night and give them presents. Now the Easter rabbit has completely taken over from the original hare.

Try making an Easter Rabbit from a balloon covered in papier maché

1. Blow up a balloon and cover with Vaseline.

2. Place in a flower pot and cover with papier maché. Apply three layers.

3. When dry cut the balloon in half.

4. Cut ears, nose, teeth and whiskers from paper and use a cotton wool ball for its tail.

An Easter Calendar

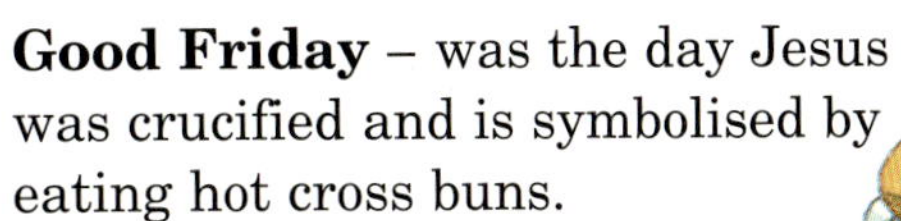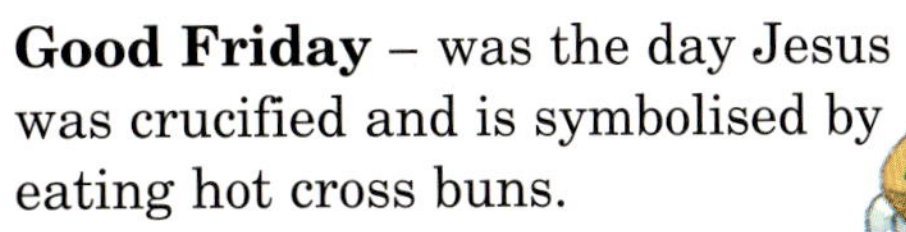

Shrove Tuesday – (or in Scots Fastern's E'en) is the day before Lent. All the rich foods were eaten up, so pancakes and oatcakes were made to use up the eggs.

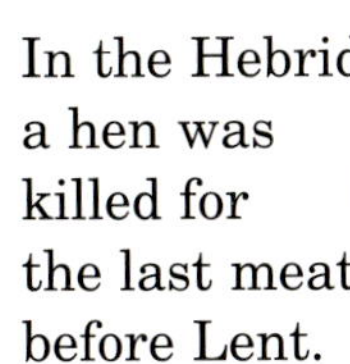

Good Friday – was the day Jesus was crucified and is symbolised by eating hot cross buns.

In the Hebrides a hen was killed for the last meat before Lent.

Easter Sunday – celebrates the resurrection. There is an old belief that at sunrise on this day, the sun dances with joy.

Mothering Sunday – takes place on the 4th Sunday of Lent. Traditionally young people who worked away from home were allowed to visit their families before the Easter festival and they took home special presents to their mothers.

Maundy Thursday – was the day Jesus shared a Last Supper with his disciples.

Passover – is the Jewish festival of thanksgiving and falls around the same time as Easter in the Christian Calendar. It commemorates when the Jews left Egypt where they had been slaves under the Pharaohs. The Passover food eaten tells its own story. The unleavened bread represents their haste in escaping from Egypt, when they did not wait for the dough to rise. Foods containing yeast are not eaten. The house is cleaned from top to bottom and special plates and cutlery are used during Passover. Families gather together for a Passover meal or Seder.

Palm Sunday – reminds Christians how Jesus rode into Jerusalem on a donkey and how he was welcomed by people waving palm branches.

SPRING FESTIVALS

Whuppity Stourie, Lanark

This is called after Whuppity Stourie, traditionally a bad fairy in Scotland. Held on 1 March, it was a children's festival. Every child held a tightly rolled ball of paper, attached by a string. As the church bells struck 6 o'clock, they whirled the paper balls around their heads and rushed around the outside of the church three times. This was to chase away the bad spirits which travelled in clouds of dust (stour), and sometimes spoiled the spring crops.

Hunt the Gowk (April Fool)

No one knows the exact origin of this spring custom, but 'gowk' means both 'cuckoo' and 'fool' in Scots. (We remember this if we say someone is a bit cuckoo, or a bit daft.) What is well known is that all huntegowks (or tricks or practical jokes) have to be played before noon on 1 April. If you played a huntegowk later than noon, children used to chant:

Kate Kennedy Procession, St Andrews

This is a colourful procession headed by a first-year male university student, dressed up as Kate Kennedy. Kate was the niece of Bishop Kennedy, founder in 1450 of St Salvator's College in the university. 'Kate' is chosen in great secrecy and 'her' identity is carefully concealed until the morning of the procession. Kate and her uncle, the bishop, ride out at the start of the procession in a carriage. There follows a blue-robed figure representing St Andrew, holding the saltire flag. Various other historical figures follow, all of them with university connections – and all making up a colourful historical pageant. There is a Kate Kennedy Ball at night for the students.

Links Market, Kirkcaldy

Held on the sea-front esplanade in mid-April, this is one of the largest street fairs held in Scotland. The site is sealed off to traffic, and travelling showmen and stall-holders play to the crowds for a whole week. The entire esplanade is brilliantly lit up, and can even be clearly admired from the other side of the Firth of Forth.

BELTANE – 1 MAY

The Celtic New Year fell in May and was one of the four main feasts of the year. Candlemas, Beltane (now Whitsun), Lammas and Martinmas were the other feast days and these are still called the Quarter Days in Scotland. They were lucky days for setting out on a journey or for a new undertaking. Holy and healing wells were meant to be particularly effective on Quarter Days. In many places there was a Beltane pilgrimage to one of these.

1 May is still celebrated in Edinburgh by people climbing Arthur's Seat and washing their faces in the May dew. If gathered before dawn, the dew has magical powers, not least giving beauty to the face washed in it. (The dew of Beltane morning was the most sacred of all water forms to the Druids.)

Also in Edinburgh there is a revival of the Beltane Fire Festival, with revellers gathering on Calton Hill to watch the May Queen and her torch-bearing attendants, and listen to the Lord of Misrule shouting out the Beltane Toast.

Beltane marked the time when the cattle were driven out to pasture from their winter quarters. In some parts of Scotland sprigs of rowan were tied with red threads to the cows' tails – to protect them from ill. Rowan was the great protector on the eve of Beltane, when fairies and other uncanny creatures were eager to do mischief. At Beltane, farmers often made offerings of food on hill-tops to birds of prey and to wild animals which might otherwise harm their livestock.

Apart from Arthur's Seat in Edinburgh, there are many traces of Beltane sites all over Scotland, including: Kinnoul Hill, Perth; Tinto Hill, near Lanark (the place of fire); Ben Ledi, Perthshire; and the great stone circles of Callanish in Lewis and Stenness in Orkney.

A recent May festival is Mayfest in Glasgow. It has a wealth of stunning events and is expanding in size every year. Look out for the children's events in their programme.

COMMON RIDING / RIDING OF THE MARCHES

Long ago, King David I of Scotland wanted to encourage his subjects to become traders. He encouraged them to build towns, or burghs. He gave his burghs special rights and trading privileges, in order that the town's burgesses would become prosperous.

One of the burgh's most important rights was its lands. In those days the burghs had to feed themselves. So they were granted common lands. The burgesses – and only the burgesses – were allowed to grow crops and to graze their sheep and cows here. The burgh's common lands had clear boundary marks to divide them off from neighbouring landlords. Often these markers were cairnstones. Every year, the burgesses rode out on horseback to inspect their lands and boundaries, and check that no stray farmers were encroaching on to their territories.

This is the basis of the Common Riding ceremony. Nowadays it is a symbolic and festive occasion when the local community reasserts its identity. Originally, it was a more serious – even sometimes warlike – event.

In a town like Lauder, the burgh charter dates back to 1502. The Lauder Common Riding takes place on the first Saturday in August, and starts early in the morning outside the burgh Tolbooth. Here the town banner is handed over to the Cornet (elected annually for the event), who promises to return it undamaged after riding round the town's boundaries. Led off by the Cornet, the Cornet's Lass, and their right-hand men and left-hand men (their guards), the horseback procession then clatters off to ride round the bounds of the town. One of the ancient cairnstones is still visited.

Today the occasion is ceremonial, so there are frequent stops for refreshment. The pubs, hotels and cafes are open from 7 o'clock in the morning, and the whole neighbourhood turns out for the event. The town is decked out with bunting. Road traffic is diverted away from the town centre.

On the Sunday before the Common Riding, there is a Kirking of the Cornet service in Lauder Parish Kirk.

Many Border towns have a ceremony of this sort. There are lots of local variations, often incorporating historical events from the area's stirring and sometimes bloody history. Mock battles between the callants (lads) are a feature of the ceremony in Hawick. Also paraded there is the Hexham pennant, trophy of a border raid into England. The Battle of Flodden is commemorated in the Selkirk Riding. Annan, Lockerbie, Langholm, Duns, Jedburgh, Kelso, Coldstream and Berwick also have a Common Riding ceremony.

Has your town got a coat of arms? Can you make a pennant from it?

SUMMER FESTIVALS

There are countless festivals, fairs and gala days in the summer months throughout Scotland – each in its own way celebrating the season and making the best of warmer weather for outdoor events. However, as our climate is extremely fickle, it is not unknown for midsummer ski-ing to take place. In 1994 the Nevis Range, near Fort William, organised a barbecue on the mountain to celebrate the fresh midsummer snows!

The rituals of Midsummer Day were similar to Beltane in past times, with bonfires lit on the hill-tops. The ancient stone circles in Orkney were used for sun worship and there were many omens of love and marriage.

Some events to watch out for are:

St Magnus Festival in Orkney which has a lot of music and drama.

Bon Accord Festival in Aberdeen includes concerts, sporting activities and piping competitions. There are also festivals in Dundee and Stirling.

Marymass Saturday in Irvine (mid-June) commemorates the presence of Mary, Queen of Scots, in 1563, before the Battle of Langside. A Marymass queen and her four attendants are a more recent addition to the 800-year-old festival. Robert Burns attended the Marymass races and it is still a favourite day out in the west of Scotland.

Guid Nychburris Festival in Dumfries (Good Neighbours) celebrates with athletic meetings, a pageant, and riding of the marches.

Bannockburn Day, Stirling (mid-June) reminds us of the heroic battle of Robert the Bruce against Edward II in 1314.

Peebles Beltane Festival; Melrose Summer Festival; Greenlaw Festival Week; Jethart Callants Festival, Jedburgh; Newcastleton Traditional Music Festival; Duns Summer Festival; St Boswells Fair; Traquair Fair; Hawick Summer Festival are some of the main festivals in the Borders Region.

There is so much happening in the way of events at this time that it is impossible to list them all individually. Most importantly this is the time to look out for your own local festival, fair or gala day. Keep a check in your local paper.

The statue of King Robert the Bruce at Bannockburn.

FISHING FESTIVALS

There is a wonderful variety of maritime museums around our coastline – from an 18th-century fishing Bod (house) in Lerwick, birthplace of Arthur Anderson, co-founder of the P & O Company; to Eyemouth in Berwickshire, home of a beautiful tapestry to commemorate a fishing disaster in 1881 when 189 local fishermen were drowned during a great storm.

The harvest from the sea was just as vital as the harvest from the land. Fishing was hard work, and often dangerous. The fishing communities had many superstitions, lots of them connected with the Bible. For example, fishermen never sailed on a Sunday. Boats were blessed at the beginning of the fishing season, but the minister was not allowed aboard the boats. It was considered unlucky to whistle on board, or to have crewmen with red hair. Certain names were not mentioned, except by code words. Here are a few – can you match the names below to their code words on the right?

Another unmentionable word was salt. There is a story from the beginning of the 20th century of a Scottish boat which ran out of salt. A crewman hailed a passing English boat thus: 'We need something that we dinna want to speak about.' The English skipper wasn't superstitious, and shouted back: 'Is it salt ye want?' When the Scots crew heard the fateful word, they all fled terrified below decks!

At home, the colour green was unlucky. You could not wear it, or have it in the house. A fisherman going to board his boat would never turn back if he had forgotten to bring something with him – that would be unlucky.

The modern fishing industry may have changed drastically from the old days. But there are still traditional gatherings at Eyemouth in Berwickshire, with its Festival of the Herring Queen at the end of the herring season, and at St Monans in Fife, with its Sea Queen Festival.

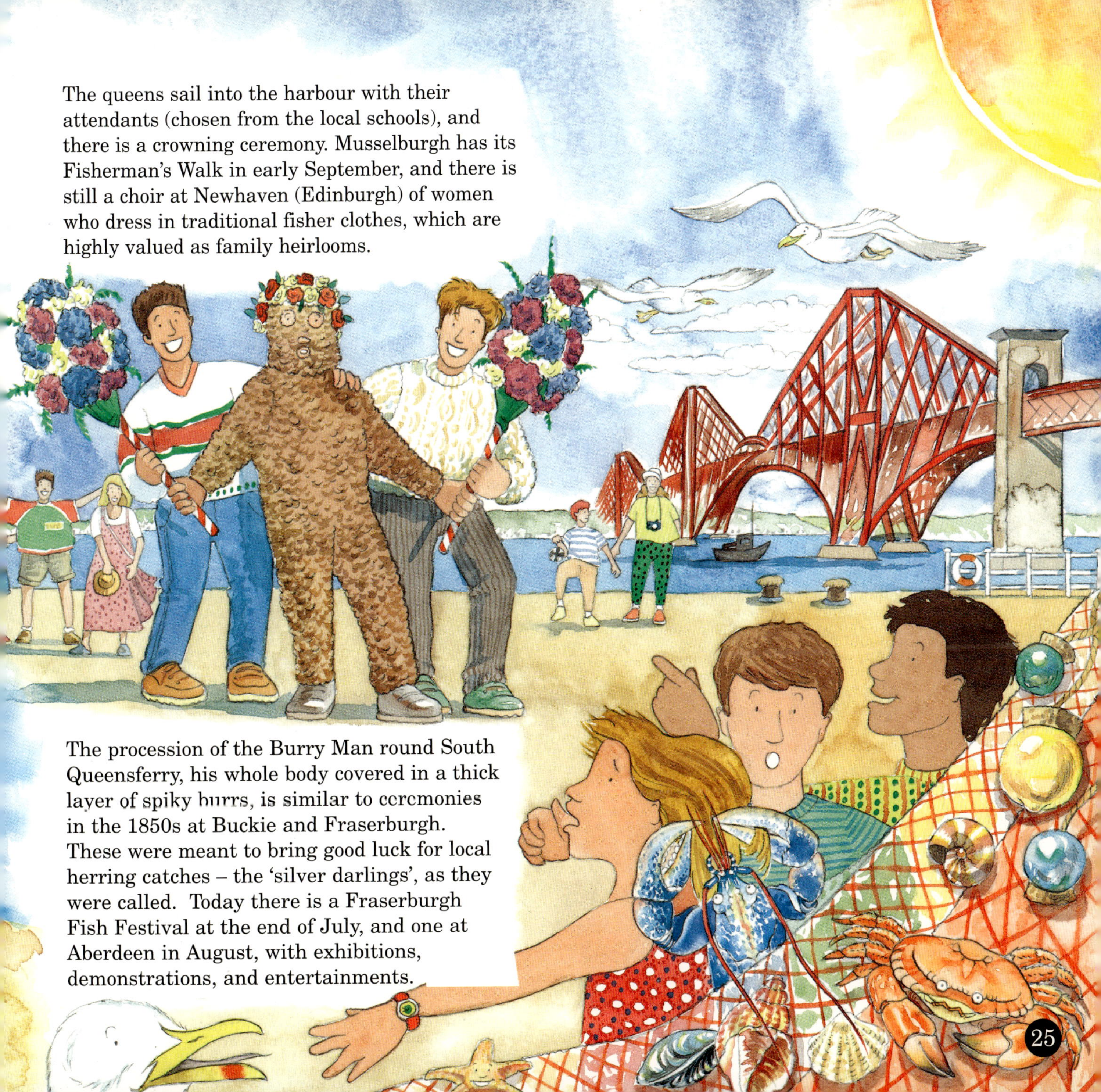

The queens sail into the harbour with their attendants (chosen from the local schools), and there is a crowning ceremony. Musselburgh has its Fisherman's Walk in early September, and there is still a choir at Newhaven (Edinburgh) of women who dress in traditional fisher clothes, which are highly valued as family heirlooms.

The procession of the Burry Man round South Queensferry, his whole body covered in a thick layer of spiky burrs, is similar to ceremonies in the 1850s at Buckie and Fraserburgh. These were meant to bring good luck for local herring catches – the 'silver darlings', as they were called. Today there is a Fraserburgh Fish Festival at the end of July, and one at Aberdeen in August, with exhibitions, demonstrations, and entertainments.

HIGHLAND GAMES

About sixty of these popular and colourful events nowadays take place all over Scotland though their origins are mostly Highland. The season reaches its height in August and early September. Some of the most famous games are held at Aboyne, Braemar, Lonach (all Aberdeenshire), Dunoon, Glenfinnan, Glenisla, Inverness and Crieff.

The Highland Games became popular when Queen Victoria and Prince Albert started attending the Braemar Gathering in 1848. This event usually takes place on the first Saturday in September. It still enjoys faithful royal support, so there is usually a big turn-out of spectators.

The oldest Games in Scotland is not strictly a Highland Games at all. It is the Ceres Games in Fife. In 1314, after the Battle of Bannockburn, the villagers held a sporting gathering here to celebrate the safe return of their 600 bowmen. It is said that these Games have been held annually ever since, without any break except for the two World Wars.

Nowadays a Highland Games usually follows a certain format, with 'heavy events' to test competitors' strength and 'light events' to test their speed and fitness. Then there are piping and dancing events, wrestling, and a tug-of-war. Pillow fights are popular, and audience

participation is often invited from those who fancy their chances. There are sometimes also shinty matches and sheepdog trials.

The best known heavy events are throwing the hammer and tossing the caber. The hammer event dates from the days of the blacksmith's forge, when young apprentices tested their strength by competing at throwing the hammer furthest. The caber event dates from the time when Speyside foresters had to toss large logs well into the river, so that the stream would carry them downriver to the sawmills. In some Games if no one can toss the caber, a section is sawn off until it can be thrown.

The light events were sprinting, walking, pole-vaulting and jumping. One of the most popular events is the hill race, in which competitors run to the top of the nearest high hill and back down again. According to a famous legend, King Malcolm Canmore (1057 – 1093) organised one of these hill races at Braemar in the 11th century.

Clan chiefs of old encouraged all these tests of speed and strength to see which of their clansmen were best fitted to act as their personal bodyguards or messengers. Even today most Highland Games have a chieftain in charge of the events and the judges.

The opening parade of a Highland Games is usually a colourful event, as are piping and dancing competitions. Highland dress is worn by many competitors.

Lammas Day – 1 August

Lammas Day was one of the four Scottish Quarter Days, once very important for people who had to pay their rents or receive their wages quarterly. The other Quarter Days were Candlemas (2 February), Whitsun (15 May) and Martinmas (11 November).

The name Lammas means 'loaf mass', when the grain harvest was celebrated and a loaf of bread was presented in the church. So it was an early version of Harvest Thanksgiving.

But the Lammas ceremony had much older, pre-Christian echoes as the Celtic festival of Lugnasa dedicated to the sun-god Lug. It was a day of feasting and thanksgiving for mercies received – good catches from the sea, good hairsts from the land. But it was not a day for dancing; because on quarter days the fairy folk went abroad, and they were much attracted to dancing.

So Lammas was really a very old pagan feast day or festival, with Christian overtones, with legal overtones, and with magical overtones. Till recently, it was thought to be a day for omens, good and bad. It was a time for burning hilltop fires, and a time when shepherd lads took a ladybird in their hand and repeated the old rhyme:

Lady, Lady Lanners
Lady, Lady Lanners
Tak yer cloak aboot yer heid
An flee awa to Flanners.
Flee ower frith and flee ower fell,
Flee ower pool and rinnin well,
Flee ower muir an flee ower mead,
Flee ower leevin, flee ower deid,
Flee ower corn, flee ower lea,
Flee ower river, flee ower sea,
Flee ye east or flee ye west,
Flee til her that loves me best.

Think of one or two things that might bring you good or bad luck if you did them on Lammas Day.

Inverkeithing's Lammas Fair has a Hat and Ribbon Race, originally for herdsmen, dating back to the 17th century. The race is preceded by a pipeband procession, with a local official carrying the decorated top hat, with ribbons for his lass. The burgh records of 1652 describe the event as a day of 'fun, frolic, fit races, ale, and drunken folks.' King James IV bought horses at the Inverkeithing Lammas Fair.

Once upon a time, everyone knew when Lammas was. In the words of the old ballad of the Battle of Otterburn:

It fell about the Lammas time
When the muir-men make their hay,
The mighty earl of Douglas rode
Into England to catch a prey....

Lammas was always a season for fairs. Three surviving Lammas Fairs are at St Andrews, Inverkeithing and Kirkwall. The St Andrews Fair and Market have been around since medieval times. Nowadays it is a noisy bash, with circus stalls and travelling tradesfolk setting up shop in Market Street and South Street. This may lead to the complete obstruction of motor transport, but it at least keeps up the colourful atmosphere of yesteryear.

EDINBURGH FESTIVAL – AUGUST / SEPTEMBER

For many visitors to Scotland, the highlight of the Scottish festival calendar is the Edinburgh Festival. It takes place over three weeks in August/September and is such an established event that people are often surprised to learn that it started only in 1947.

The original idea was to celebrate the return of peace after the dark days of World War Two. From small beginnings, the Edinburgh Festival has grown into the world's biggest cultural event – bringing a feast of music, film, theatre, jazz, art, and books to the city.

The sheer size of the Festival can be a problem. How can anyone get around all the events? In 1992, there were 550 companies performing 1196 shows, in over 110 venues. And that was only on the Fringe, which is the name for the 'Unofficial Festival'!

The Festival also brings a very special holiday atmosphere to Edinburgh – to remind us that festivals are about people enjoying themselves, being entertained and amused. Its full name is the Edinburgh *International* Festival, and it has become a very cosmopolitan event. Performers flock in from all parts of the world, as do visitors. The streets of the city take on a carnival atmosphere, and there are street entertainers – from pipers and pavement artists to fire-eaters and stiltwalkers – wherever you go.

Native Scots enjoy the Festival most for bringing artistic events from overseas to their attention, while visitors can learn about Scotland's own culture. The pubs and hotels, the restaurants and gift shops, the taxi drivers and tour guides of Edinburgh do a roaring trade.

Some of the most spectacular events are held in the open air. Weather permitting, the fireworks display over the Castle, or the Military Tattoo on the Castle Esplanade are dazzling affairs. Holyrood Park becomes the world's biggest open-air sideshow for a relaxed couple of weekends, often with hot-air balloons overhead.

The old idea of a festival thus lives on: it is an opportunity to forget your worries and problems, to be diverted and entertained.

Write a letter to your favourite author, asking him / her to come and talk at one of the Edinburgh Book Festival events.

Edinburgh schoolchildren compete every year to produce the posters with which the city will advertise its Festival. Could you design one? Or maybe one for your own home town?

Harvest (Hairst)

People have given thanks for a good harvest since earliest times. This was the season when a whole year's work came to a head. The first sheaf of corn was offered to the gods to ensure a good harvest for the next year. The last sheaf (the Maiden or Clyak) was thought to house the spirit of the corn. A corn dolly (Kirn-dolly) was made from this, then hung in the kitchen until the New Year when it was either burned or ploughed back into the field.

The privilege of cutting the last sheaf of corn – for it brought good luck to the cutter – was often given to the most attractive or youngest girl on the field. Before mechanical reapers were invented, the harvest was cut by hand. The main tool used was the heuk or sickle. Squads of reapers started with the Berwickshire and Lothian harvest, then followed the ripening crops through Fife and Central Scotland to the west. A custom at the end of the cutting was for each reaper to take his sickle by the point and throw it over his shoulder. The way it landed predicted the reaper's fate for the next year.

When all the corn was harvested, the harvest-home (or kirn) celebrations could begin – a welcome break in the toil for farm workers, whose only other holiday in Scotland used to be at New Year!

In the 19th century a special church Thanksgiving was started. Churches today are decorated with sheaves of corn, vegetables, fruit and flowers for their harvest festivals. Schools often have their own services and follow the tradition of distributing the produce to the sick and elderly in the neighbourhood.

Did you know?

The full moon occurring nearest to the autumn equinox (21 September) is called the Harvest Moon. As the angle of the moon's path to the horizon is minimal at this time, the moon rises at the same time for the next few nights – not 5 minutes later each night, as it does normally.

Try making a straw picture. Soak straw stalks in water. Slit them open and flatten them. Make patterns, or shapes, then glue them onto card.

HALLOWE'EN–31 OCTOBER

This was the night before the old church feast of All Hallows, or All Saints' Day. In the even older Celtic Calendar before the Christian era it was called Samhuinn, or the Feast of the Dead. Samhuinn was one of the two great Celtic fire festivals (the other one was Beltane, or May Day).

Why dooking for apples?

This ritual seems to go right back to pre-Christian times. Before a dead soul could rest in peace, it had to go through several 'trials', including a Trial by Water. Hence the bucket of water. Why apples? Because the name of the island of Blessed Souls was Avalon, which also meant 'the island of apples'.

Why bonfires and turnip lanterns?

Two thousand years ago people believed that dead spirits came back to haunt the living during the Feast of the Dead. So they lit lanterns to guide the spirits back to the spirit world. The scooped-out turnip was given a spooky, skull-like face to frighten away evil spirits.

The big bonfires were originally burnt at dusk to combat the powers of darkness and the coming of winter. Ballad writers in the Middle Ages described how 'the mirk and midnight hour' was the really spooky moment, when the spirit world was briefly upset, and when the fairyfolk left the Other Country and rode abroad among humankind. The passage between the two worlds could be two-way: for sometimes humans were spirited away by the fairies to the Other World at this time of year!

Why guisers?

Guisers were people who dis**guised** themselves so that the spirits of the dead would not recognise them. To be recognised by the dead spirits meant getting trapped in limbo – stuck between this world and the next world. This was a terrifying fate.

So even today, when children come guising to your door with false masks and turnip lanterns, you must pretend not to recognise them – even if you know who they are.

Why trick or treat?

Again, this goes back to the spirit world. The spirits could be good to you, if you treated them with proper caution and respect. But they got up to all sorts of pranks if you offended them, even if you didn't mean to upset them.

Tramp, tramp, tramp, the boys are marchin,
We are the guisers at the door.
If ye dinnae let us in
We will bash yer windows in,
An ye'll never see the guisers any more.

Why witches?

Traditionally, witches were no more than bad fairies. So they too were very active at this time, like all the other spirits and fairyfolk. They were said to fly through the air on their broomsticks or gallop over the lonely moors on their black horses.

St Andrew's Day – 30 November

St Andrew is the patron saint of Scotland. He was a fisherman in Galilee and became one of the first disciples of Jesus. Later he preached the gospel in Greece and Southern Russia. When he was martyred, he did not think himself worthy of the cross of Christ, so he chose a different shape of cross – a saltire.

It is believed that some of his bones were brought to Scotland 1600 years ago. A Greek abbot, Regulus, was visited by an angel who told him to take some of the saint's bones, sail west with them, and build a shrine wherever he came ashore. Regulus did so, and eventually landed at what is now St Andrews on the coast of Fife. The shrine he built is now covered by the site of the cathedral.

Today the festival of St Andrew's Day is celebrated all over the world where Scots gather together for a special dinner, recite poems, and enjoy Scottish singing and dancing.

Interesting Facts

St Andrews Cathedral was the largest ever built in Scotland. Most of it was destroyed by fire in 1378.

The white cross of St Andrew was easily seen to be different from the red St George's cross in battle. Scottish troops were ordered to wear the saltire on front and back in battle so that they could not be mistaken for English troops.

St Andrew is also patron saint of Greece, Romania and Russia.

The West Door was the main processional doorway used by the canons.

The St Andrew cross used to be on the Russian naval ensign. If the Czar of Russia wanted to honour someone, they were made a member of the order of St Andrew.

SPOT the DIFFERENCE

The St Andrew cross, or saltire, is the national flag of Scotland. In 1707 it became part of the Union Flag, when the Scottish and English parliaments were joined together.

What is the difference between the Union Flag and our present Union Jack?

Christmas / Yule – 25 December

Until recently, Yuletide was not celebrated in Scotland to the same extent as Hogmanay. The ancient feast of Yule lasted from 25 December till 6 January – the twelve days of Christmas. Yule comes from an old Norse word *jol* – a Scandinavian festival of the winter solstice. This was 21 December, when the sun is at its greatest distance below the equator; we often call it 'the shortest day'.

There have been midwinter festivals from the prehistoric days when people worshipped the sun – long before Christmas was celebrated. The Church eventually decided to celebrate the nativity or birth of Christ on an official date. Midwinter was thought to be a good time, when people couldn't do much work on the land. Christmas is thus only part Christian; many midwinter pagan rituals remain linked to this festival.

Christ's Mass, or Christmas as it became known, was once a much longer festival lasting from Christmas Eve until Candlemas Day (2 February). People prepared for the nativity of Christ at Advent, four Sundays before Christmas. Our celebrations now end on the Twelfth Night (6 January). This is the Christian feast of Epiphany, when the baby Jesus was shown to the Three Wise Men who were to spread the news of his birth.

Design your own Guid Yule card for sending to a friend. Use a Scots greeting inside:
Biddin ye a blyth yule tide an a guid new year.

Christmas customs

Yule log

The rekindling of fire on the hearth or altar was an important part of the feast of Yule. A little of the log was burnt on each of the twelve days of Christmas.

Christmas cards

Invented in 1841 by Charles Drummond, a publisher in Leith. By 1880 the Postmaster General had to issue the first 'Post Early for Christmas' message.

Santa Claus

This name comes from St Nicholas, a bishop in the 4th century. He gave away a large fortune left to him, to help the poor. He is the patron saint of Aberdeen, where the parish church is named after him, and where there are several local festivals connected with him. The festival of St Nicholas is actually 6 December. On that day long ago, the rector of Aberdeen Grammar School dressed one of his pupils up as the saint, and sent him around the town collecting funds. Today in Aberdeen, the saint rides down Union Street on a sleigh.

The Christmas tree

The decoration of trees during the midwinter festival was originally a pagan rite. The custom was revived in Britain by Queen Victoria's husband, Prince Albert. The tree erected on the Mound in Edinburgh each year is a gift of thanks from the people of Norway for help given to their country in World War Two.

The holly and the ivy

Both the Romans and the Norsemen decorated their houses with evergreen to symbolise perpetual life in the dead days of winter. Scots share the folk tradition which says that Christ's crown of thorns was made from holly – and the berries, once white, were stained with his blood. In Scotland it is thought unlucky to burn holly or step on the berries.

Mistletoe

The Celts thought of this as a sacred plant. The custom of kissing under the mistletoe comes from a Norse legend – an arrow made from mistletoe wood killed Baldur, the god of light. Thereafter the old gods made the plant look on while people kissed!

Twelfth night

Traditionally this is the night of 5–6 January, when Christmas decorations are taken down and Christmas comes to an end. Yuletide used to be celebrated on 6 January in some parts of the Highlands, in accordance with the old calendar. The change from the Julian to the Gregorian calendar in 1752 was much resented by country people. For many, Auld Yule (6 or 7 January) remained the real day of celebration, especially in the Northern Isles. It is still observed with Auld Yule dances on 7 January, especially in Shetland.

PLACES TO VISIT AND ANSWERS

There are many new heritage museums opening up around Scotland. Watch out for any developments in your local area. Here are some of the places that are well worth a visit. Always check opening times before visiting.

1. Aberdeen Maritime Museum,
Aberdeen 01224 585788

2. Alford Heritage Centre,
Alford, Aberdeenshire 019755 62906

3. Almond Valley Heritage Centre,
West Lothian 01506 414957

4. Angus Folk Museum,
Glamis, Angus 0130 784 288

5. Auchindrain Museum of Country Life,
near Inveraray, Argyll 0149 95 235

6. Bannockburn Heritage Centre,
Bannockburn, Stirlingshire
01786 812664

7. Braemar Highland Heritage Centre,
Braemar, Aberdeenshire
013397 41944

8. Buckhaven Museum,
Buckhaven, Fife 01592 260732

9. Buckie Maritime Museum,
Buckie, Moray 01309 73701

10. Burns Cottage and Museum,
Alloway, Ayrshire 01292 41215

11. Land o' Burns Centre,
Alloway, Ayrshire 01292 43700

12. Dunaverig Farm Museum,
near Thornhill, Stirlingshire

13. Eyemouth Museum,
Eyemouth, Berwickshire
018907 50678

14. Fife Folk Museum,
Ceres, Fife 0133 482 380

15. Gairloch Heritage Museum,
Gairloch, Ross-shire 0144 583 243

16. Highland Folk Museum,
Kingussie, Inverness-shire
01540 661307

17. The Hirsel,
Coldstream, Berwickshire
01890 882834

18. Landmark,
Carrbridge, Inverness-shire
0147 984613

19. Lossiemouth Fisheries Museum,
Lossiemouth, Moray

20. Newhaven Heritage Museum,
Newhaven, Edinburgh
0131 551 4165

21. North-East Scotland Agricultural Heritage Centre,
Mintlaw, Aberdeenshire 01771 22857

22. Orkney Farm and Folk Museum,
at Corrigall, Harray and Kirbuster, Birsay

23. Royal Museum of Scotland,
Edinburgh 0131 225 7534

24. St Andrews Cathedral,
St Andrews, Fife 01334 72563

25. Scottish Agricultural Museum,
Ingliston, Edinburgh
0131 225 7534

26. Scottish Maritime Museum,
Irvine, Ayrshire 01294 78283

27. Summerlee Heritage Park,
Coatbridge, Lanarkshire
01236 31261

28. Timespan Heritage Centre,
Helmsdale, Sutherland 014312 327

29. Wick Heritage Centre,
Wick, Caithness

Answers:
Page 24:
salmon: redfish; pig: grunter; minister: sky pilot; rabbit: map-map.